Diana Dolman.

Bought in Beijing (Peking) 1988 for 35 YUAN
(approx £5.30 ENG.)

中國貴州少數民族服飾圖案藝術

ETHNIC COSTUME FROM GUIZHOU

Clothing Designs and Decorations from Minority Ethnic Groups in Southwest China

by The Nationalities Affairs Commission of Guizhou Province
The Folk Art Gallery of Guizhou Province
The Provincial Museum of Guizhou

FOREIGN LANGUAGES PRESS   BEIJING

First Edition   1987

ISBN O-8351-1738-3

Copyright 1987 by Foreign Languages Press

Published by Foreign Languages Press
24 Baiwanzhuang Road, Beijing, China

Distributed by China International Book Trading Corporation
(Guoji Shudian), P.O. Box 399, Beijing, China

Printed in the People's Republic of China

Contents

The Artistic Features of Costume Decorative Patterns of Ethnic Groups in Guizhou Province

By HUANG SHOUBAO
DIRECTOR, FOLK ART GALLERY, GUIZHOU PROVINCE

Costume decoration is an art closely linked with people's daily life. There is a rich and long standing wealth of this art in China, especially among the national minorities, each of whom retain their own artistic features. The Miao, Bouyei, Dong and Shui nationalities in mountainous Guizhou Province, southwest China, have created magnificent patterns for the decoration of their national costumes. Those patterns are indeed some of the brightest flowers in the luxuriant garden of Chinese folk art.

Since ancient times, the ethnic groups in Guizhou have been living in the mountains on the Guizhou plateau in a picturesque landscape and fine climate. In their long history, they have created a colourful and varied folk art, an important component of which is their costume decorative art. The patterns used by each ethnic group on their costumes retain striking features peculiar to the group. They vary even among people of the same ethnic group owing to their differences in locality, customs and habits. Those who live on plains and valley areas prefer long skirts and loose jackets with broad sleeves, whereas those high on the mountains wear tight clothes with narrow sleeves and short skirts or trousers. The 2.6 million Miao people in the province are scattered in the various mountainous areas in all parts of the province, and their difference in location can easily be distinguished through their garments and hairstyles, as well as the designs, colours and compositions of the decorative patterns on their kerchiefs and clothes. This has given rise to an admirable diversity of decorative costume patterns among the national minorities in Guizhou.

The decorative patterns on the garments of the minority peoples in Guizhou generally retain the techniques of weaving, embroidery, hand-stitching and dyeing traditional among the Chinese people. Weaving is done on simple hand looms to create patterns on the basis of warps and wefts of different colours. Embroidery is done by hand on cloth, with patterns freely stitched with either silk or cotton threads. Hand-stitching is done to create patterns by making numerous stitches in the meshes formed by warps and wefts to form a series of tiny x's and -'s. Wax dyeing is more complicated. Molten wax is first applied on a piece of cloth to make a pattern. The cloth is then dyed and the pattern appears after the wax is bleached. In putting the patterns on the garments, women of the national minorities do not stick to one technique only, but often choose one technique as the main one and complement it with another technique to meet the actual needs in life as well as their own artistic tastes. For instance a decorative pattern is done mainly by weaving but can be augmented with additional decorative elements by embroidery. Or a piece of wax dyed work is enriched by some auxiliary embroidered designs, or hand-stitching is blended with embroidery. Combinations of the techniques make the patterns more exquisite and heighten the national characteristics of the works.

One salient feature of the costume decorative art among the national minority peoples in Guizhou is the considerable contrast of the decorations with the garments they embellish.

The garments are generally black or white and the decorations are designed and made to be added to suit the parts of the garments they decorate. These decorative pieces are often made independently. For example, the piece added to the front of a skirt is called "yaowei," or apron. A piece sewed on a carrying pad is called a carrying pad piece. Similarly, pieces put on sleeves, the bottoms of trousers and the hems of jackets all have their own names. Making decorative patterns on separate pieces to be sewed on different parts of garments is a practice peculiar to the ethnic groups in Guizhou. Such small decorative pieces are easy to make and can be used as gifts among friends and relatives. Therefore women have quite a number of decorative pieces with which they change the decorations on various parts of their clothing from time to time. This enables the women to keep their dresses always fresh looking. Meanwhile, this practice has also made it possible to preserve a wealth of costume decorative patterns among the minority peoples through the generations and to facilitate the collection and study of this decorative art.

Another feature of the costume decorative art among the ethnic groups in Guizhou is that the artists who make the superb decorative patterns are just average working women. They make the decorations not for sale but solely to satisfy their own aesthetic sense in relation to their actual needs in life. They therefore may give free rein to their creative imagination, which gives their works a

spontaneous and untrammelled character in both content and style. In the national minority areas in Guizhou, people judge the industry and cleverness of a young woman on the basis of the costume decorative patterns she makes. And young men choose their girl friends by looking at their decorative patterns.

In this context, little girls start learning the skill of making decorative patterns from their mothers or grandmothers and young women must work hard to make their own dowry,

especially the decorative patterns on carrying pads, well before their marriages. Through this, they not only express their desire for happiness, but also display their talent and deftiness. Many exquisite decorative pieces are works by young women. When you visit a national minority village in Guizhou, the hospitable hosts often show you the beautiful decorative pieces made by the female members of the families. "We like the beauty of peacocks and we would like to dress ourselves as prettily as them. There are so many beautiful flowers on the hills, birds in the trees, clouds in the sky and rainbows after rain. Nature is so varied and beautiful. We want to catch the beauty of Nature and put it on our skirts and jackets." These are some of the remarks by young girls when they talk about their artistic creations.

The contents of the decorative patterns are motifs based mostly on images the women are familiar with in their daily life, such as birds and beasts, fish and insects, flowers and domestic animals, cottages and carts. There are also such traditional auspicious designs as lions playing with balls, dragons with pearls, phoenixes gathering around peonies and mandarin ducks playing on water. In addition, each ethnic group has its own traditional designs, such as checkers representing farmland, wavy lines indicating rivers and crosses symbolizing trees. These conventionalized patterns have been preserved from generation to generation. What is particularly worth mentioning is a spiral pattern which has been passed down as a sacred sign. It takes an outstanding position in the costume decorative art of the ethnic groups in Guizhou.

The shapes of the designs show that the artists resort mainly to traditional Chinese techniques of line treatment instead of using light and shadows. Images are framed out with lines and the most outstanding characteristics of an object are often brought out by images like silhouettes. However, the women artists refuse to fetter their imagination by holding to the actual shapes of objects. They abstract and idealize the images by additions, reductions, exaggerations and distortions. They achieve a harmonious blend of variations with the help of thick and thin dots, long and short lines, big and small sides, and realistic and surrealistic images.

In the use of colours, the women artists seek a strongly sensuous and exuberant effect. They like contrasting colours but in actual application, contrasts in colour are applied only on small areas to keep variety of colour in harmony. Meanwhile, either very deep or very light background and bold lines of frames are used to bring the numerous colourful patches into a pleasing unity. This treatment of colour is capable of melting even patches of loud colours into the whole to form a pleasant looking picture, a happy marriage of gaity with quietness, elegance with brightness.

In composition, the costume decorative patterns of the Guizhou national minorities do not emphasize the subjects and the proper treatment of the relationship between the subject and the auxiliary, although there are variations in density of the images. Most of the patterns fill up the whole pieces of cloth with more or less an even spread of the designs. This is perhaps out of the need of achieving an effect of wholeness on a garment. Extensive use is made of symmetry, balance, radiation and a reciprocity between the central and corner figures to make the costume decoration attain a special artistic appeal.

What is amazing is that the extremely rich variety and beauty of the costume decorative patterns is created by the labouring women of the minority peoples with just a few needles, embroidering threads, small wax knives and simple hand looms on crude home-spun cloth. But the sweat and talent of these women has added numberless exquisite works of art to the treasury of art of mankind. This is something the national minotity people in the southwest China province of Guizhou can be proud of.

2. A young Miao woman embroidering a long apron.

Embroidery

Embroidery dates back to more than 4,000 years ago in China. Embroidery, which gives the artist a broad scope for artistic conception and talent because of its contrast to the texture of the cloth, has found extensive applications in the decoration of national costumes among the ethnic groups in Guizhou Province, especially in districts where the Miaos and Dongs live in compact communities in the southeastern part of the province. National minority women in Guizhou generally embroider on patterns of paper cuttings fastened to the cloth instead of on patterns painted on it. The paper cutting designs are either the works of paper cutting artists or made by the embroiderers themselves.

The different techniques of embroidery have resulted in different features of the embroidered products. Flat embroidery with split strands of colour threads, for example, produces a brilliant lustre and brightness in the colours. Embroidery with threads of a string of tiny knots brings out an effect of vigour and boldness. And embroidery with plaited strands of threads has an effect of freshness and simplicity. All these techniques are popular among Guizhou minority peoples. An embroidery technique called "horse-tail embroidery" is popular among the Shui people in the province. Horsetail hair with white embroidery thread wound round it is used to stitch out the outlines of a pattern and then embroidery silk is embroidered inside the frames according to the pattern. Works with "horse-tail embroidery" make the patterns stand out in relief.

Women of the Dong nationality sometimes plan their patterns on a number of pieces of base cloths and embroider a part of the pattern on each of the pieces and then put them together to create a diversified pattern.

This great variety of embroidery techniques among the national minority peoples in Guizhou is determined by the varied contents and artistic images. People draw on rich imagination from their work and daily lives and make artistic generalizations from it. Young women resort to artistic approaches that use exaggerations, stylizing and abstraction to create auspicious dragons and phoenixes, birds in pairs, flowers in full bloom, lovely fish and insects, wonderful cottages, human figures and domestic animals. What is worth mentioning is that the human figure takes a predominate

3. Miao girls begin learning costume decorative art as early as in their childhood. Picture shows an elderly lady teaching two kids how to embroider.

position whenever it appears in a design. The human figure may not be very large in a pattern, but it always appears in a beautiful setting and takes up an important position in the picture. However, embroidery is not painting and no particular element should stand out. Each part is harmoniously incorporated into the whole. Take the apron pattern for example.

Despite variations in the images and colour schemes, the composition almost always follows the conventional practice — with the upper part comprising a round floral pattern in the centre and flowers in the corners and the lower part comprising four narrow stripes and three broad ones placed alternately. This conventional composition brings out a strong national and local style. In all the patterns, the embroiderers do not base the images on the actual sizes, postures, colours and life cycles of the animals and plants but create them according to their own artistic conception and the requirements of the composition. This gives their decorative art a romantic touch.

What is peculiar to embroidery of the national minority people in Guizhou province is the addition of auxiliary ornamental articles. The Miao people use small pieces of thick golden cardboard, copper or glass. These ornamental pieces are generally round in shape, occasionally triangular or square. They are sewed to the patterns either to fill blank spots or form lines to heighten the brightness of the patterns. When young women dance on holidays, their embroidered costumes with such ornaments glitter in the sun.

4. A young Miao lady in elaborately embroidered costume.

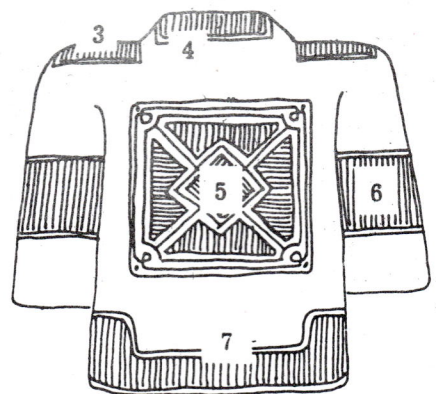
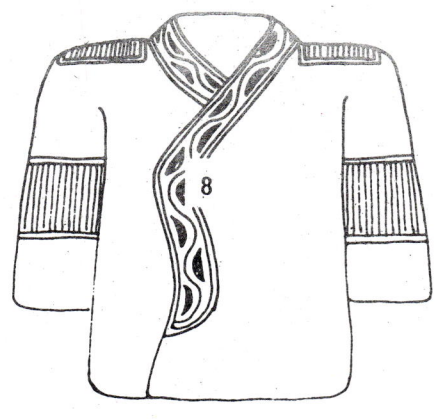

Names of the Parts of
Garments for Decorations:

1. Carrying pad, used by mothers for carrying babies on their backs

2. Centre piece of a carrying pad

3. Shoulders

4. Collar

5. Back of a jacket

6. Sleeves (showing the middle section of the sleeves)

7. & 8. The hems of a garment

9. Apron (to be fastened round the waist over a skirt)

5 A Miao mother with her baby in a carrying pad.

6. A pattern of a pair of mandarin ducks playing on water embroidered on the centre piece of a carrying pad which is used by a mother to carry her baby on her back. The mandarin ducks, almost always seen in pairs, are widely used by Chinese folk artists as a motif symbolic of lasting love and happy marriage. (*Shui nationality*)

7. The geometric pattern of an embroidered centre piece of a carrying pad. The square is made up of triangles of varying sizes and shades of colour. On the triangles are patterns of butterflies, flowers, fish and birds which form a lively and well-balanced unity. (*Miao nationality*)

8. This is the upper part of a carrying pad with a pattern of butterflies lingering on flowers. The outer frame of the pattern is embroidered with horse-tail hair which is covered with twining strands of colourful threads. This makes the frame of the pattern stand out to achieve a relief effect. (*Shui nationality*)

9. A carrying pad with a pattern of happiness and longevity which is popular in Chinese folk art. (*Shui nationality*)

17

10. A geometric pattern on a carrying pad with rhombs as the basis for its composition. (*Miao nationality*)

12. The pattern of dragon and fish on a carrying pad. It is an embroidered piece on patchwork with pieces of cloths of different colours — a happy blend of simplicity and elegance. (*Shui nationality*)

11. A geometric pattern on a carrying pad. (*Miao nationality*)

13. & 14. Patterns of butterflies and flowers on carrying pads. Embroidery is done on patchworks with cloths of different colours, a much more elaborate work than patchwork using the same cloth. The overall effect of the pattern is striking while on each small part there is embroidery. (*Miao nationality*)

16. This circular floral pattern on a carrying pad is put together with separate embroidered pieces. (*Dong nationality*)

15. A circular floral pattern on the centre piece of a carrying pad of the Dong nationality. Dong embroidery is characterized by a richness in colour and a neatness in composition. Tiny mirrors are often used to add brightness to the embroidery. (*Dong nationality*)

17. A geometric pattern on the back of a costume. (*Ge people*)

18. A pattern of butterflies and flowers on the shoulders of a costume.(*Miao nationality*)

19. A rhomb pattern of dragons on the back of a costume.(*Miao nationality*)

20. A net pattern on the back of a costume. The subdued pattern and dark colour, which are not common for Miao embroidery, are adopted generally by the elderly. (*Miao nationality*)

21. A geometric net pattern on the back of a costume. (*Miao nationality*)

22. A pattern of flowers and birds on the sleeves of a costume. This composition of stripes is a conventional pattern in Miao embroidery on sleeves. (*Miao nationality*)

23. A pattern of birds and beasts on sleeves. The pattern, consisting of sections each embroidered in a different colour, achieves a lively effect. (Miao nationality)

27

24. A dragon pattern on sleeves. The conventional practice is to place the dragon amid clouds. Miao women, however, make the dragon slither amid flowers. (*Miao nationality*)

25. A pattern of a lion playing with a ball on sleeves. Every stitch is not drawn to the full. This type of embroidery with loose stitches of colour strands is called crease-stitch. (*Miao nationality*)

26. A sleeve pattern of birds and beasts. In Chinese folk art, the pomegranate signifies a multitude of children and the word beast is pronounced as *shou*, the same for the pronunciation of the character longevity. The use of the pomegranate and beasts is a reflection of the hope for many children and longevity. (*Miao nationality*)

27. A sleeve pattern of peaches and pomegranates. Glistening pieces are usually placed in blank spaces between patterns in Miao costume embroidery, but the glistening pieces on this are stitched amid patterns to enhance the artistic effect. (*Miao nationality*)

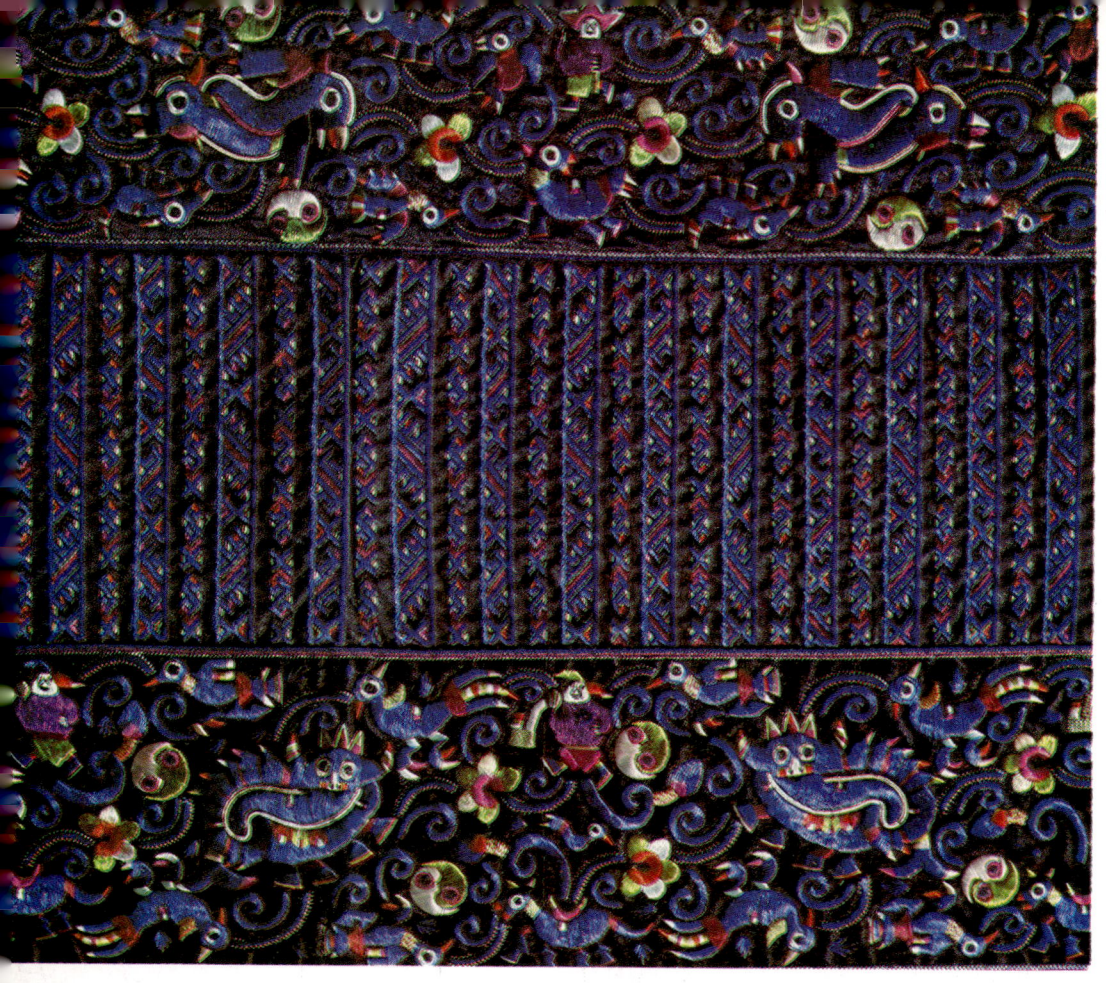

28 , 29. & 30. These three sleeve patterns of flowers, birds, insects and butterflies are similar in composition but different in colour scheme to suit the tastes of women of diverse age groups. (*Miao nationality*)

31, 32. & 33. These three geometric patterns on the sleeve belonging to the category of scattered design are done with flat stitches in embroidery. (*Miao nationality*)

34. & 35. Sleeve patterns of dragons. The dragons are highly stylized to transcend the conventional concept of dragons. (*Miao nationality*)

36. This sleeve pattern of a boy and two dragons comprises strikingly coloured patches embroidered with thick threads of several strands together. This shows one of the basic embroidery techniques peculiar to the Miao nationality.

37. A sleeve pattern of chicken-like dragons showing a child in front of the door watching two dragons with heads like those of chickens fighting. (*Miao nationality*)

38. A sleeve pattern of dragons and phoenixes. Young Miao women show a daring in thinking by creating dragons of heads of cats, tails of phoenixes and feather crowns. (*Miao nationality*)

39. A sleeve pattern of rhombs. (*Miao nationality*)

40. An apron pattern of fish and dragons. The apron patterns of the Miao nationality usually are composed of rhomb-shaped multi-layer floral patterns on top of flowers in between stripes to achieve an effect of unity. (*Miao nationality*)

41. An apron pattern of fish and dragon. In Chinese folk art, dragons and snakes are usually seen slithering amid clouds. This pattern, however, romantically presents the dragon together with fish and frogs. (*Miao nationality*)

42. An apron pattern of two dragons vying for a magic ball while butterflies hover and birds sing around them. (*Miao nationality*)

43. A stylized dragon pattern for aprons. (*Miao nationality*)

44. A geometric pattern used on shorter aprons. (*Miao nationality*)

45. & 46. Apron patterns of double dragons and double phoenixes. The colourful patterns are outlined by white silk threads to achieve a vivid effect. (*Dong nationality*)

47. The corner design of an apron pattern with butterflies and flowers. (*Dong nationality*)

48. A round floral pattern for aprons. (*Dong nationality*)

49. A collar pattern of birds and flowers. The design, consisting of a sunflower flanked by phoenixes and butterflies with a lovely baby in the centre of the sunflower, conveys the artist's love for life. (*Miao nationality*)

50. A shoulder pattern of flowers and birds. (*Miao nationality*)

51. A dragon and buffalo pattern for the shoulders of a costume. The dragon, which is associated with water and the buffalo, which is associated with the earth, symbolize a good farming year of excellent weather and hard work — traditional aspirations of the farmers. (*Miao nationality*)

52. A pattern of continuous rhombs used on the hems of a jacket.(*Miao nationality*)

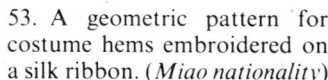

53. A geometric pattern for costume hems embroidered on a silk ribbon. (*Miao nationality*)

54. A dragon and phoenix pattern used around the bottom of trousers. To meet the requirements of the strip shape, the artist ingeniously lengthens the tails of the phoenixes and the bodies of the dragons. (*Dong nationality*)

55. A round floral pattern on a child's cap. Bright flowers are embroidered on three pieces of cloth which form a "roof" with tassels hanging down from both sides. (*Dong nationality*)

58, 59, 60. & 61. Pillow patterns of dragons, phoenixes, flowers and birds. The two ends of pillows are embroidered with different patterns like traditional Chinese paintings of the fine-stroke school. The designs are both decorative and lively. (*Bouyei nationality*)

57. A floral pattern for decorating a waistcoat. (*Yi nationality*)

56. A pattern of round flowers covering the shoulders of a costume. The pattern consists of lotus and pomegranate flowers, tigerheads and bats. The bold lines give an effect of paper-cuts. (*Dong nationality*)

62. A floral pattern on shoes. (*Dong nationality*)

63. A young Miao woman weaving a band on her weaving bench (a simple loom).

Weaving

Almost every household in villages and hamlets of national minority people in Guizhou boasts a very simple loom. The air vibrates with the rhythmic click-clack of the looms early in the morning and late in the evening and often the rhythmic sounds mingle with young women's ringing songs floating out from the villages. The young women dye and starch cotton or silk yarns into different colours and weave them into aprons, carrying pads, kerchiefs, bags and quilt covers. They call their products "tapestry."

The woven products by the Miao and Dong peoples enjoy the greatest renown among the ethnic groups in Guizhou. Such woven pieces all have exquisite patterns which women weave without making designs in advance. They just complete the patterns while weaving on the loom according to the traditional techniques passed down to them orally from the older generation or based on their own artistic imagination.

There are certain differences between the Miao and Dong tapestries.

When Miao women weave an

apron, they use uniform white or blue warps and colourful wefts and the wefts are broken up whenever a change of colour is required. The weaver separates the warps with a slip of bamboo for the shuttle to go through once and then makes another separation of the warps for another weft to be put through. The process is repeated slowly as the pattern requires the use of wefts of different colours. The tapestry thus woven has a bright pattern on one side only. Work progresses slowly. An apron about 70 centimetres long usually takes several months to finish.

The Dong people occasionally adopt colour patterns. Generally they just weave patterns of black and white or blue and white. The warps are black or blue and the wefts are white. Geometric patterns are woven on both sides, only with opposite colour schemes. For example, if the pattern on one side is of a light colour tone with white the dominating colour, then the other side is of a dark colour tone with blue or black the dominating colour. This tapestry with a light colour on one side and a dark colour on the other is peculiar to Dong tapestry. This method not only gives a varied effect to the product but also avoids cleverly the usual dull colouring of black and white patterns.

In addition, a portable loom is also used by women of national minorities in some places in Guizhou. Women can bring portable looms to the fields and resume weaving during work breaks. The weaver ties the end of the warps to her toes and fastens the other end to her waist. She weaves a narrow band by handling a simple shaft manually.

The interlacing of weaving produces continuous geometric patterns which give a neat and varied effect at the same time. But

64. Dong women in their holiday best ready to go to a fair.

the patterns differ because of differences in weaving techniques. The tapestry of Miao people often adopts geometric patterns of dragon and phoenix images. The patterns are complicated and the colour is as bright as the weaver desires. The Dong tapestry may also present a great range of patterns by compositions with just the two colours of white and black (or blue) augmented by grey, which is formed by the interlacing of black and white threads. Although the colour scheme is simpler for Dong tapestry, the contrasting two colours in a harmonious composition have the charm of simplicity.

67. This pattern of rhomb-shaped flower and bird designs on carrying pads is common in the embroidery of the Bouyei nationality. (*Bouyei nationality*)

65. & 66. Miao women weaving waistband and kerchief material.

68. This rhomb-shaped pattern on a carrying pad has an effect of harmony, rhythm and variety. (*Dong nationality*)

69. A rhomb-shaped pattern on a carrying pad. The composition of rhombs of different sizes and light, elegant colours forming a harmonious tone is peculiar to the weaving technique of the Bouyei nationality. (*Bouyei nationality*)

70. A pattern of square-shaped chrysanthemums on a carrying pad. (*Bouyei nationality*)

71. A multi-layer square-shaped pattern on the bands of a carrying pad. This pattern using a plain-coloured square design in the centre surrounded with bright frames is a salient feature of the embroidery of the Dong nationality. (*Dong nationality*)

72. & 73. Geometric patterns on the bands of carrying pads. (*Dong nationality*)

74. & 75. Rhomb-shaped patterns on bands of carrying pads. The rhombs of varying sizes are woven into the bands with warps and wefts of different colours. (*Miao nationality*)

76. & 77. Patterns of continuous rhombs with flowers show superb weaving skill to achieve a perfect blend of rhythm and variety. (*Miao nationality*)

78. A net pattern encompassing highly stylized galloping horses and flying birds represents the unique style of the band weaving of the Dong nationality. (*Dong nationality*)

79. A rhomb-shaped pattern for bands on carrying pads. By lining the main rhombs with continuous rhombs on both the upper and lower sides, the pattern gives a close-knit rhythmic uniformity. (*Dong nationality*)

80. A geometric pattern for the "chicken feather apron." It is so called because hanging from the hem of the geometrically patterned apron are strings of bead-like seeds of wild plants with feathers of chickens dangling from the strings. (*Dong nationality*)

81. & 82. Apron patterns of dragons and phoenixes with images of dragons, phoenixes and lions neatly arranged in three rows of rhombs to achieve an effect of depth and variety. (*Miao nationality*)

83.&84. Apron patterns of dragons and fish. Surrounding the dragons and fish are also human figures, horses and birds. (*Miao nationality*)

85. & 86. Apron patterns of scattered geometric figures. (*Miao nationality*)

87. & 88. Apron patterns of dragons and phoenixes. (*Miao nationality*)

89. Continuous rhomb patterns on collars woven with silk and cotton threads. (*Bouyei nationality*)

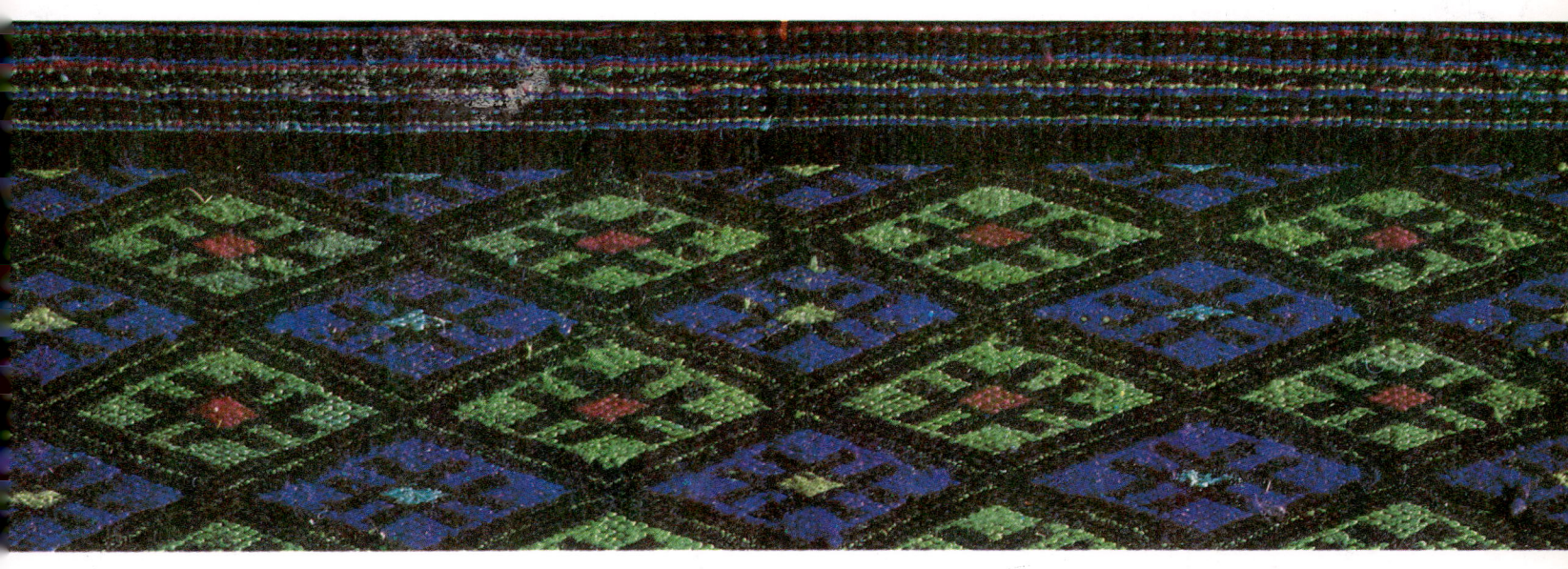

90. & 91. Rhomb-shaped hemline patterns. Miao women take the flowers of wild pears which dot the hills in spring as motifs to make geometric patterns in their weaving to retain a strong native flavour. (*Miao nationality*)

92. Young Miao women are making holiday costumes of hand-stitching work in spring.

Hand-Stitching Work

Hand-stitching is a branch of embroidery produced by making stitches between the two nearest meshes of the fabric. Patterns are thus formed by the numerous cross stitches or "-" stitches.

Hand-stitching is extensively applied to the decoration of clothes and other daily use articles. The costumes of the Miao women in the Huaxi region of Guizhou are almost entirely decorated with hand-stitched patterns. They learn the skill early in their girlhood. Very often they create patterns on the fabric without preparing sketches in advance. They just put on the cloth designs stored in their memory or created in their minds' eye.

The technique of hand-stitching is divided into positive stitching and negative stitching. the former is done with the pattern on the upper side of a piece of cloth as the stitches are made from the upper side. This method is easier to learn but consumes more time than negative stitching. The latter is done with the back side of the cloth facing the embroiderer and with stitches made from this side while the pattern is formed on the other side, which is the front side of the piece of cloth. This method has the advantage of looking at the movements of the stitches at the back side of the cloth, thus making the work progress faster and the pattern on the other side prettier. But it requires greater proficiency, which is acquired only after long practice.

The composition of hand-stitching patterns is generally made up of straight lines to forming symmetrical patterns. The compositions may fall into the following categories:

One is formed by cross-stitches of dark cotton or silk threads on white cloth. The patterns are generally those of flowers, birds, butterflies and domestic animals. They are found mostly on bridal kerchiefs. Young women often work with heart and soul to make a design of "the bridegroom riding a horse to meet his bride" before a wedding.

Another is done with coloured cotton or silk threads on blue or red cloth. Cross-stitches of different colours fill up a pattern, leaving only the frame of the pattern unstitched to reveal the background of the cloth. This type is generally done by negative

93. A Miao girl is seen engrossed in her hand-stitching work.

stitching to show a pattern on the positive side. This composition may contain a broad range of such motifs as clouds, flowers and birds, dragons, phoenixes, lions and tigers. The compositions are complicated and rich and the colour schemes varied.

One more type of hand-stitching is the "-" stitches popular in some districts of the province. This type of hand-stitching is different from the simple and spontaneous style of the black and white stitching, and from the magnificent colour stitching. Works of such stitching appears to be embroidery at first glance. A closer look, however, reveals a continuously circling movement of stitches. Patterns done with this type of stitching on the backs of clothing look like brocade.

94. A girl dressed in a beautiful hand-stitched costume from Huaxi on the outskirts of Guiyang, a well-known centre of hand-stitching work.

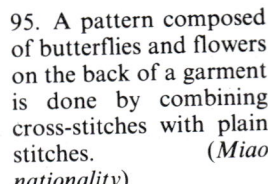

95. A pattern composed of butterflies and flowers on the back of a garment is done by combining cross-stitches with plain stitches. (*Miao nationality*)

96. A geometric pattern incorporating images of flowers, ripples on a pool and swimming fish. The lively design breaks the usual monotony of geometric patterns. (*Miao nationality*)

97. A geometric pattern for a carrying pad. Variety is achieved through the employment of contrasting colours and an intermingling of different sizes of figures. (*Bouyei nationality*)

98. This geometric rhomb pattern on a carrying pad is made by hand-stitching with additional embroidered figures, which is one of the basic decorating arts of the Dong nationality on costumes. (*Dong nationality*)

99. This pattern of butterflies, flowers and vines on a carrying pad is done with colourful single threads to achieve a rich and lively effect. (*Miao nationality*)

100. A pattern of geometrically shaped phoenixes and peonies on the back of a jacket. The continuous geometric patterns done with plain stitches form a broad decorating area. (*Miao nationality*)

101. A hand-stitched geometric pattern on the back of a jacket. This is a complete pattern typical of Miao hand-stitching for its close-knit layout and exquisite stitches. (*Miao nationality*)

102. A geometrically-shaped hand-stitched pattern on the back of a jacket. Combining diagonal lines with vertical ones to form continuous, varied patterns is one of the commonest compositions in hand-stitching. (*Miao nationality*)

103. A geometric pattern on the back of a jacket. The floral patterns made up of radiating lines of varying thicknesses result in a rhythmic composition. (*Miao nationality*)

104. A butterfly-flo
pattern on the back
jacket. (*Miao nationa*

105. A geometric patte
with wavy lines on
back of a jacket. (*M.
nationality*)

106. A geometric network pattern on the back of a jacket. The sporadically placed bright colour against a subdued background enhances the vitality of the design. (*Miao nationality*)

107. A geometric sleeve pattern comprising flying birds and butterflies arranged in rhombs, triangles and stripes. (*Miao nationality*)

108. A floral pattern of honeysuckle for sleeves. The uniform yet varied composition is achieved by carefully placing the flowers, which are linked together by plain stitches. (*Miao nationality*)

109. Strip-floral patterns on sleeves. (*Dong nationality*)

110. A pattern on a diaper. The Miao people like silver ornaments. Since silver ornaments are too heavy for babies, young mothers make hand-stitched diapers with a design of silver ornaments (here a silver lock) on it. (*Miao nationality*)

111.112. The skirts of Dong women are made of dozens of bands which are woven with different patterns. At the end of each band is a tassel of beads with feathers hanging down from them. (*Dong nationality*)

113.114. A geometrical pattern of birds, fish and butterflies on kerchiefs hand-stitched with black silk thread. (*Dong nationality*)

115.116. Round floral patterns of unicorn and spotted deer on kerchiefs. Those were traditionally considered to be auspicious animals. The compact compositions are achieved through adding flowers and butterflies around the unicorn or the deer. (*Dong nationality*)

117. A composition of auspicious patterns on a kerchief which incorporates into a harmonious unity a baby riding a unicorn, surrounded by lions, deers, vases and flowers. (*Dong nationality*)

118. This is a wedding kerchief hand-stitched with a round pattern of phoenixes amid poenies in the centre and sedan chairs with brides surrounded by butterflies—creating a picture of rejoicing. (*Dong nationality*)

119. 120. Round floral patterns on kerchiefs hand-stitched with human figures, horses, chariots, birds and flowers which are used commonly by Dong women. (*Dong nationality*)

121. A floral pattern on the hem of trousers. (*Miao nationality*)

122. A butterfly-flower pattern on stockings. (*Miao nationality*)

123. Ge girls making designs for wax dyeing. Ge people are a subdivision of the Miao nationality in China.

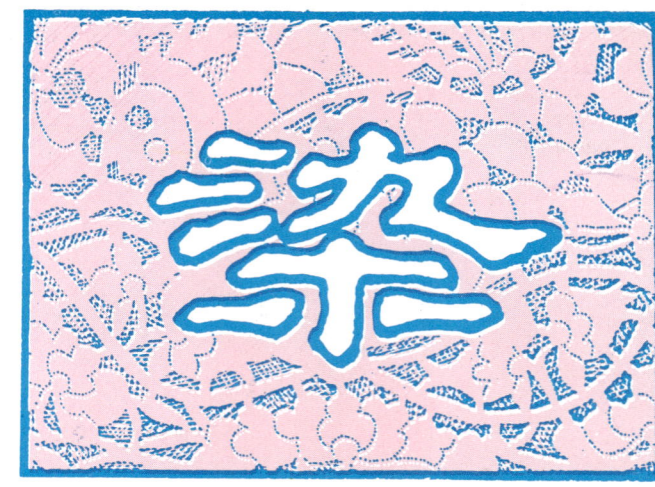

Wax Dyeing

124. Copper knives—tools for making wax dyeing designs.

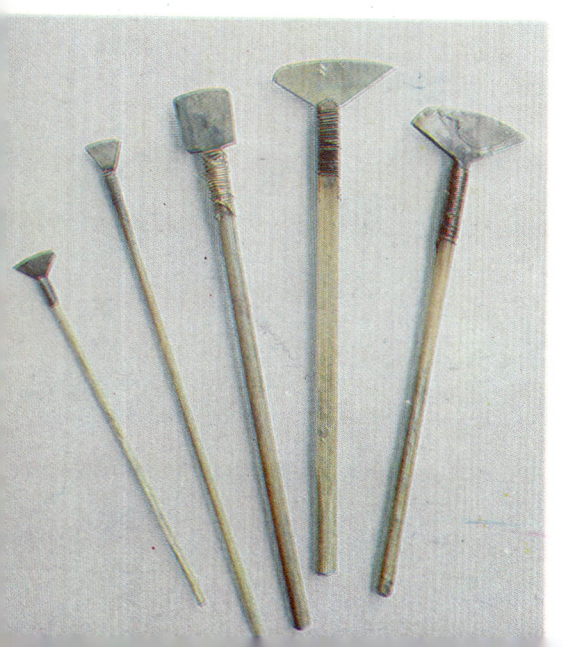

Wax dyeing is a folkcraft art that dates from the days of ancient China. It is used extensively and skillfully by ethnic groups in Guizhou Province. *The Annals of Guizhou* records that "Cloth is painted with wax and dyed. After bleaching, the pattern looks like the work of embroidery." Figures dressed in clothes decorated with wax dyed patterns are found on the murals of the Dunhuang Grottoes and the Tang Dynasty painter Zhang Xuan's works. Historical data indicate that the wax dyeing art in the central part of China has come from the mountainous regions of Southwest China. It is estimated that wax dyeing dates from an even earlier period.

Wax dyeing is divided into the two processes of painting and dyeing.

In painting the pattern, one first melts beeswax in a porcelain cup over a low fire, dips copper knives in it, scratches the outline of a pattern on a piece of starched cloth with the fingernail and then paints a pattern with the molten wax. Success lies in skilfully handling the wax knife and maintaining the optimum temperature of the wax to ensure the fluency of the strokes.

Dyeing is done by soaking the wax-painted cloth in a jar filled with a dye solution prepared from a plant. Five or six times of dyeing baths are necessary before the cloth is placed into boiling water to bleach out the wax. The finished product retains the pattern in white. The dye solution must be kept to a specific density. When it becomes lighter after several dyeings, more dyestuff has to be added. When more than one

shade of colour is desired, after one or two dye baths, the cloth should be dried and those parts that are to receive the lighter colour should be painted with molten wax before further dyeing is done. Should other colours such as red and yellow be added to blue, then the parts to be dyed red or yellow should be waxed first, leaving out only the parts to be dyed in the blue dye solution. Similarly in dyeing the parts in red, all the rest of the cloth has to be waxed before dyeing. The blue, red and yellow dyestuffs are all made from indigenous plants.

Painting pattern with wax is an art young women of national minorities in Guizhou must master. They start learning the art when they are six or seven years old and are already very skillful

when they are in their teens. By the time they marry, each has already prepared for herself several wax-dyed pieces of garments. This practice is rather prevalent in Miao and Buyi communities. However, differences in customs and localities result in different compositions of the wax-dyed patterns, which roughly fall into the following three categories:

The first type is patterns of motifs taken from nature such as those of flowers, birds, insects and fish. These images are created with flowing lines to achieve an artistic effect instead of copying the actual shapes. For example, when a bird is painted, the artist may position the bird's head, tail, claws or wings in a way in compromise with the round

125. Ge people doing dyeing.

126. Rinsing after dyeing.

shapes. At a glance, such a composition, like an abstract painting, is at variance with nature. But it is not difficult to appreciate the creative imagination.

The second type is mainly geometric in composition. Patterns of swivels, clouds, waves and zigzags are composed with complexity, neatness and variation. Although highly abstract, they are based on inspiration by things that exist in nature. Take the spiral patterns for instance. Some people say they represent whirlpools in the streams. Others believe they are the images of a kind of life-saving medicinal herb and still others say that they represent the marks on the crown of the oxen. All these beliefs indeed reveal people's reminiscences of their labour and their desire for better lives. Such patterns that convey people's good wishes have been passed down through the generations.

The third type is a happy blend of geometric designs with images of things in nature. The mixture of the designs in composition, enhanced by a multitude of colours and additional embroidery, create extremely exquisite patterns. Wax dyeing of the national minority peoples is a long-standing tradition that is truly a gem in the treasure house of folk arts in China.

127. 128. 129. These three floral patterns on carrying pads are of a similar composition but the designs at the centre are different. (*Miao nationality*)

130. 131. 132. The round floral patterns on carrying pads feature interlocking figures pivoting on the central figure, which has been a traditional approach of the Ge people in their wax dyeing designing.

133.134.135. Round floral patterns of flowers, birds, insects and fish in a harmonious composition. These patterns are on carrying pads. (*Ge people*)

136. Patterns of small round designs on the back of a costume. The patterns of clouds are intermittently arranged with embroidered round floral patterns and on both sides are two strips of embroidery to form a vivid symmetry. (*Ge people*)

137. Spiral and cloud patterns on the back of a costume. Precision and neatness of the lines are the key to success for such designs, which can be executed by only experienced hands. (*Ge people*)

138. A flower and bird pattern on a kerchief. The freely arranged figures give the design the strong flavour of a traditional Chinese painting. (*Miao nationality*)

139. A flower and bird pattern on a kerchief. (*Ge people*)

140. A cloud pattern on a kerchief. The picture of contrasting blue and white is obtained after several dyeings of the cloth printed in rice starch with a pattern board. (*Ge people*)

141. A cloud pattern on a kerchief. (*Ge people*)

142. A pattern of scattered flowers on a diaper. (*Miao nationality*)

143. A geometric pattern on sleeves. (*Ge people*)

144. A geometric pattern on sleeves. (*Miao nationality*)

145. A colourful floral pattern on sleeves. (*Miao nationality*)

146. A geometric pattern on the hems of a jacket. (*Ge people*)

147. A geometric pattern on the shoulders of a
jacket for a young man. (*Miao nationality*)

149. A wax-dyed jacket
(*front*). (*Ge people*)

148. A pattern on an
apron of the Ge people.

151. A wax-dyed jacket.
(*Miao nationality*)

150. A wax-dyed jacket
(*back*).(*Ge people*)

99

152. A spiral pattern on skirts. (*Bouyei nationality*)

153. A colour floral pattern on shoulder pads. (*Miao nationality*)

154. A spiral pattern on sleeves. (*Bouyei nationality*)

155. A zigzag pattern on sleeves. (*Bouyei nationality*)

SKETCH MAP OF DISTRIBUTION OF SOME OF GUIZHOU'S
MINORITY NATIONALITIES

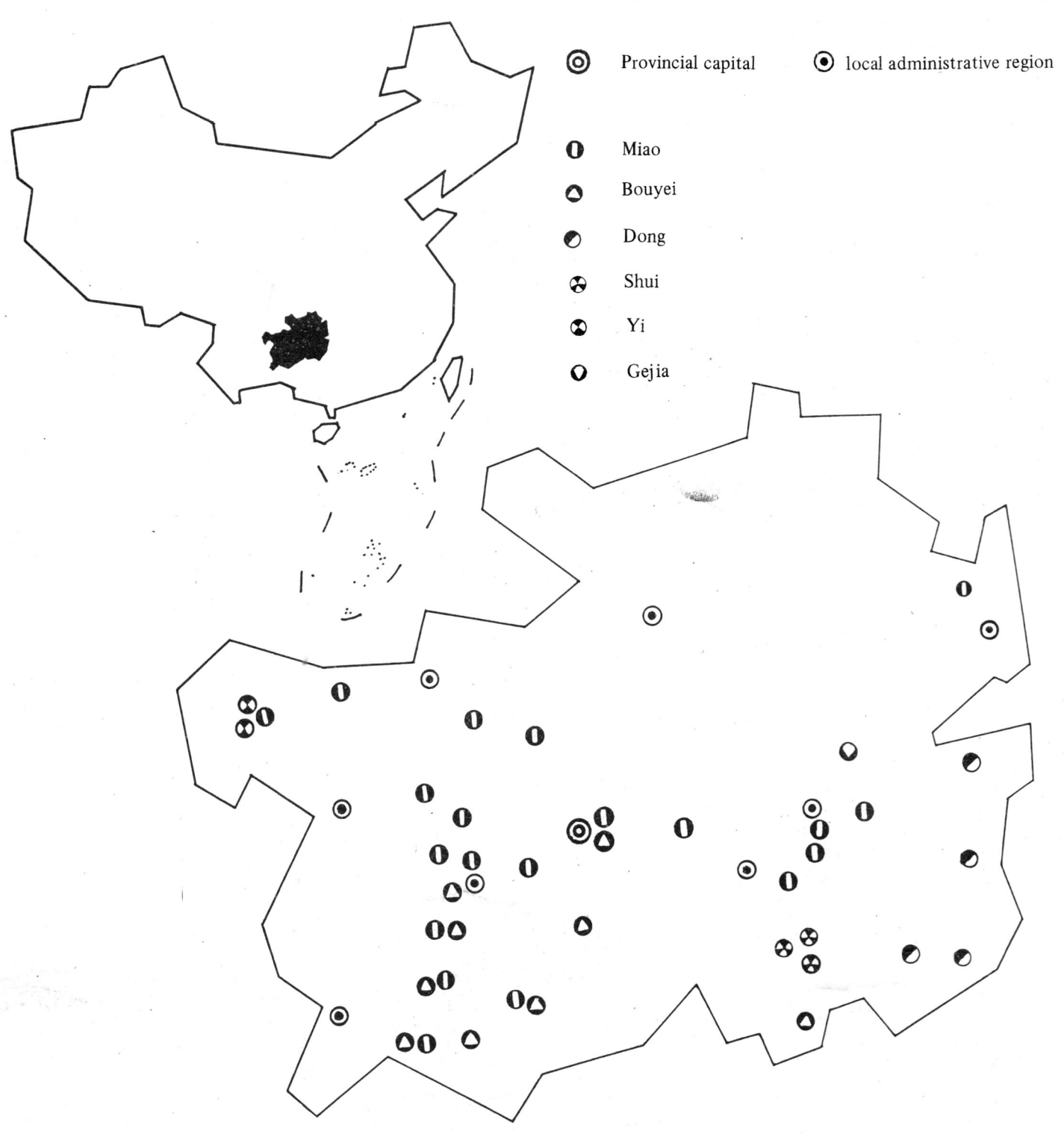

贵州少数民族服饰图案艺术

编辑： 黄守堡　刘宗河

摄影： 吴仕忠

*

外文出版社出版
（中国北京百万庄路24号）
天津静一胶印厂印刷
中国国际图书贸易总公司
（中国国际书店）发行
北京399信箱

1987年（12开）第一版

编号：（英）8050－2811

03000

84－E－637 p

Compiled by Huang Shoubao, Liu Zonghe
Written by Huang Shoubao
Photographs by Wu Shizhong
Edited by Zhou Daguang
Translated by Liu Bingwen